THE SOOTHSAYER

ISBN 960-425-043-4

SIGMA PUBLICATIONS
20, Mavromihali St.,
GR - 106 80 Athens, Greece
Tel. 36.07.667, Fax 36.38.941

Folk tales from Greece

The soothsayer

By Menelaos Stephanides

Illustrated by Photini Stephanidi

Translation: Bruce Walter

Sigma Publications

Once upon a time, in a distant kingdom, there lived a lazy fellow called Cicada. All day long his wife Hazel kept on scolding him because he wouldn't go out to work and there was nothing for them to eat.

"Go and be a labourer," she would tell him.

"That's not the kind of work for me," he'd answer.

"Then be a builder," she would say.

"That's not my sort of job," Cicada always repeated.

"Become a blacksmith, then – make horseshoes."

But idle Cicada would usually give the same reply: "Those aren't the kind of jobs for me."

Another time, still yawning lazily, he came out with these words: "Just you wait and see. One day this husband of yours will be a minister of the king."

"You could be right at that," said Hazel with a mocking laugh. "In this kingdom it's types like you who get the high positions. And come to think of it, I'd rather like to be a minister's fine lady."

"No, I'll settle down and become a blacksmith after all, ha! ha!" laughed lazy Cicada. And so the time went by and he did nothing whatsoever.

One lunchtime, as he was making his way back home and wondering if there would be anything in the house for him to eat, he heard the next door neighbour shrieking that thieves had run off with her hen.

"A curse on him, whoever took it!" she kept crying, making enough noise with her wails to wake the dead.

"Hey, why all this fuss about a single hen?" Cicada asked her. And just so he wouldn't have to listen to her screaming any more, he added:

"It's fallen down the well. Drop a bucket down and pull it out. But if you find it, you will give me something for my trouble, all right?"

The neighbour ran to the well, dropped the bucket in, and when she hauled it up again, there was the hen inside, a little bedraggled, but safe and sound!

She gave a penny to Cicada, and he ran straight to his wife shouting, "Look what I've got in my hand. Off you go to get some bread for us to eat and then I'll tell you the funny thing that happened."

Hazel ran straight off to the baker's and they wolfed down the loaf the moment she got back. Then Cicada told her how he'd come to earn it.

Hazel listened open-mouthed.

"I've got it!" she cried once he had finished. "You can become a magician – a soothsayer!"

"Hm, not a bad idea at that. It rather suits me, come to think of it. But just how does one become a soothsayer? I don't know anything about telling fortunes."

"You don't have to know," replied his wife. "If others have done it, so can you. All you've got to do is look the part and put a bold face on it."

So they rummaged in an old chest, fitted Cicada out in an assortment of brightly-coloured robes, and he became a soothsayer.

The news soon spread throughout the kingdom, and one day there arrived at Cicada's door some men sent by the king to learn if the child the queen was going to bear would be a boy or girl.

They were the very last people our magician wanted to set eyes on.

"How do you expect me to put a bold face on it now?" he muttered to Hazel.

"What did you say?" the king's men asked him.

"Oh, nothing, nothing," he replied. But they pressed him to reply:

"Won't you tell us what child the queen is going to bear, great soothsayer?"

Cicada was even more terrified by now, and he began to say:

"A boy, a girl, a boy, a girl, a boy, a girl ..."

The king's men saw that they weren't going to get any sense out of him, so they gave up and left.

Shortly after this the queen gave birth – and she had not one baby but twins: a boy and a girl.

"Your majesty!" the courtiers said in surprise. "The soothsayer was right. He told us the queen would bear you a boy and a girl. He is a true magician after all." And the king did not forget this.

A few days later, the king's golden casket filled with sovereigns disappeared from the palace.

They searched the kingdom from end to end, but it was nowhere to be found.

Then the king ordered, "Bring the soothsayer to me."

Cicada was led into the royal presence with a fanfare of trumpets and the king ordered him to go and find the golden casket.

At these words, panic seized the false magician (as if there are any real ones!). But to hide this confusion, and because he was hungry, too, he asked,

"Give me a few hazelnuts and a drop of brandy wine."

"What on earth can he want them for?" the courtiers whispered among themselves.

"He is a magician," replied the king, "and he will know."

The soothsayer took the hazelnuts and the brandy and set off filled with dread. On his way, he ate a few of the nuts and told himself,

"A little nap would do me good."

These words were hardly out of Cicada's mouth when he spotted a deserted hut. And who should be sitting in it but the thieves who had robbed the king! As soon as they spotted him, they took to their heels and hid themselves. Once our magician was in the hut, he ate a few more of the nuts and drank a little of the brandy. Then he lay down on the floor and murmured, "Here comes the first one," and with a single great yawn he fell fast asleep.

What he meant was the first yawn – but one of the thieves had crept up to the door to listen, and when he heard the magician's words he fled in terror to the others and gasped,

"He knew I was there! As soon as I put my ear to the door, do you know what he said? 'Here comes the first one'. He must be a magician!"

Not long after this, the soothsayer woke up, ate a few more of the hazelnuts, took another pull at the brandy bottle and felt sleepy once again.

"Here comes the second," he said, as he yawned once more and his eyes closed.

And would you believe it – at that very moment the second thief had put his ear to the door!

"He knew I was there, too!" he ran to tell his companions, trembling with fear. "As soon as I bent down, he said, 'Here comes the second'!"

"Well, then it's my turn to go," the third thief said, but he wrapped his scarf around his head because he was afraid that the magician might recognize him.

Meanwhile, Cicada had woken up, eaten a few more of the nuts and drunk a drop or two of brandy. Sure enough, he soon felt sleepy again, but by now he was rather cold as well, so wrapping his robe around himself for warmth, he lay down for the third time and, as another great yawn escaped him, he murmured, "Here comes the third one, all wrapped up!" and fell asleep.

Scared out of his wits, the listening thief ran straight back to the others and told them,

"All is lost! As soon as I got near, he said, 'Here comes the third one, all wrapped up'!"

By now the three thieves were in despair. And being stupid, as all thieves are, they went into the hut, woke Cicada up and told him:

"We know you have recognized us for the thieves who robbed the king. If you promise not to tell on us and let us get away, we'll tell you where we've hidden the casket."

"Done!" cried the soothsayer, rubbing his hands with glee.

"It's just here. Dig and you will find it," the thieves told him.

Then the magician went and brought two soldiers. They did the digging, because Cicada, as we have seen, was a lazy fellow, and when they had got the casket up, the three of them set off for the palace.

When the golden treasure chest was opened in the presence of the king, it was filled to the brim. Not a single sovereign was missing. The king was overwhelmed with joy and placed the soothsayer beside him at the royal table. When they had eaten and drunk their fill, they went out in the garden for a stroll.

As they wandered under the trees, the king quickly plucked a cicada from a hazel bush while the soothsayer was not looking, and hid it in his fist.

"There is one more question I shall put to you", he said, "to see how great a magician you really are. I want you to guess what I am holding in my hand."

"Oh, what have I got myself into!" groaned Cicada under his breath, "My wife Hazel is to blame for everything." Then he spoke to himself aloud, in a despairing voice:

"It's your own fault, Cicada. You shouldn't have let that Hazel deliver you into the king's hands!"

The king, of course, thought that Cicada was talking about the little insect he had picked from off the hazel bush and held hidden in his fist. He was convinced by now that this was no ordinary magician. And so he placed both lazy Cicada and his Hazel among his ministers at court.

For that is how ministers were created once upon a time.